D0987233

KEVIN DURANT

BY MARTY GITLIN

Published by ABDO Publishing Company, PO Box 398166, Minneapolis, MN 55439. Copyright © 2013 by Abdo Consulting Group, Inc. International copyrights reserved in all countries. No part of this book may be reproduced in any form without written permission from the publisher. SportsZone™ is a trademark and logo of ABDO Publishing Company.

Printed in the United States of America,
North Mankato, Minnesota
052012
092012

 THIS BOOK CONTAINS AT LEAST 10% RECYCLED MATERIALS.

Editor: Chrös McDougall
Series Designer: Craig Hinton

Photo Credits: Rich Pedroncelli/AP Images, cover, 1; Eric Gay/AP Images, 4, 27; Ronald Martinez/AP Images, 7; Denis Poroy/AP Images, 8; Frank Franklin II/AP Images, 10, 14; Joe Don Buckner/AP Images, 13; Ted S. Warren/AP Images, 16; Manuel Balce Ceneta/ AP Images, 19; David Zalubowski/AP Images, 20; Sue Ogrocki/AP Images, 22, 28; Mark J. Terrill/AP Images, 24

Library of Congress Cataloging-in-Publication Data

Gitlin, Marty.
  Kevin Durant : NBA superstar / Marty Gitlin.
      p. cm. -- (Playmakers)
  Includes index.
  ISBN 978-1-61783-547-6
  1. Durant, Kevin, 1988--Juvenile literature. 2. Basketball players--United States--Biography--Juvenile literature. 3. African American basketball players--Biography--Juvenile literature. I. Title.
  GV884.D868G57 2013
  796.323092--dc23
  [B]
                          2012018280

TABLE OF CONTENTS

CHAPTER 1

GREATNESS IN ACTION

Game 6 of the 2012 Western Conference Finals was almost over. The Oklahoma City Thunder were going to win. Kevin Durant was ready to celebrate. He saw his mother and brother courtside. Kevin wrapped his arms around them. He and the Thunder were going to the 2012 National Basketball Association (NBA) Finals for the first time.

The idea seemed crazy a few days earlier. The San Antonio Spurs had beaten the Thunder in the first

Kevin Durant embraces his mother after leading the Thunder past the San Antonio Spurs in the 2012 playoffs.

two games of the conference finals. The Spurs had a lot more experience in the playoffs than the Thunder. But the Thunder had Kevin.

The three-time NBA scoring champion led the Thunder to three straight wins. But the Spurs quickly jumped out to an 18-point lead in Game 6. The Thunder again looked doomed. But Kevin again stepped up. He scored 34 points, grabbed 14 rebounds, and had five assists. The Thunder more than erased the Spurs' lead. Kevin even had time to celebrate with 15 seconds still left.

The road to greatness was tough for Kevin. He was born on September 29, 1988, in Washington DC. His mother, Wanda Pratt, and his grandmother raised him. They lived in an area outside the city called Seat Pleasant. But it was not pleasant at all. It was a poor neighborhood.

Kevin is not the only basketball player in his family. His younger brother Tony Durant starred for the Towson University Tigers. Tony has a special place in Kevin's heart. Kevin hugged his brother first when Kevin's name was called in the 2007 NBA Draft.

Kevin drives to the hoop against the San Antonio Spurs in the 2012 playoffs.

Kevin loved basketball from an early age. He worked hard at the sport. And he did not let anything hold him back. Kevin practiced eight hours per day by age 10. Seat Pleasant Activity Center coach Taras Brown did not want Kevin to play five-on-five games. Brown wanted Kevin to master the fundamentals first. Sometimes Brown made Kevin play nothing but one-on-one defense for an hour.

Legendary coach John Wooden presents Kevin, *right*, and Chase Budinger a trophy after a high school All-Star game in 2006.

Some young basketball players only want to practice shooting. Kevin would later be one of the NBA's great scorers. But he was also a top all-around player from the start.

Kevin went to National Christian Academy for high school. He started on the varsity basketball team as a freshman. Kevin only got better. He led the team in scoring the following year. He could play any position on the court. It became clear that

Kevin had special talents. So he left for Oak Hill Academy in Virginia for his junior year. Oak Hill is known for its strong basketball teams. Some experts said Kevin was the second best high school player in the United States.

Kevin then went Montrose Christian for his senior year. It is in Maryland. He averaged 23.6 points and 10.2 rebounds per game. He also showed a great work ethic. It would later help him become an NBA star.

But first he had to go to college. The NBA does not allow players to join straight from high school. So Kevin decided to go to the University of Texas. Many believed Kevin was already good enough for the NBA. He was about to prove it.

Taras Brown coached Kevin at the Seat Pleasant Activity Center. Brown made sure Kevin was in shape. So did Kevin's mother. They made him run sprints up nearby Hunt's Hill three or four times a week. Kevin later guessed that he ran the hill 1,000 times in six years.

Kevin Durant

CHAPTER 2

SHORT STOP IN TEXAS

The University of Texas is in Austin, Texas. That is a long way from Washington DC. But Durant was already famous when he got there. That is because he was already a top-rated player before suiting up for the Longhorns.

Most people believed Durant would only stay at Texas for one year. Then he could join the NBA. Fame and fortune awaited in the NBA. But Durant tried not to let his future change him. He worked hard to stay

Durant battles for a rebound with a Michigan State player during a 2006 game.

grounded in college. Durant prayed and read the Bible every night before going to sleep.

Durant was 6-foot-9. Some college centers are not even that tall. But Durant was very skilled with the ball. Texas coach Rick Barnes said Durant could have played any position. Mostly Durant was a forward, though.

College basketball is a big step up from high school basketball. Sometimes it takes a long time for college freshmen to adapt. But Durant was not like most freshmen. He was immediately the best player on the team. Some even believed he was the best college player in the country.

Durant scored at least 20 points in 11 of his first 13 games. And he was just warming up. He shined the brightest in one four-game stretch. He averaged 34 points and 14 rebounds in those games. He also made 54 percent of his shots during that

Durant was on fire when Texas played the Texas Tech Red Raiders on January 31, 2007. He had 37 points and 23 rebounds in the win. No player in Big 12 Conference history had scored more than 30 points and grabbed more than 20 rebounds in one game until then.

Durant looks to drive against Texas Tech during a 2007 game. Durant led Texas to a 25–10 record.

hot streak. Durant finished among the nation's top five in both scoring and rebounding. No other player matched that.

The Longhorns were a top team. They went 25–10. They reached the second round of the national championship tournament. People around the country knew why Texas was so good. It was because of the team's star freshman. Durant was named the College Basketball Player of the Year. No freshman had won that award before. And Durant won it easily.

The Portland Trail Blazers had the first pick in the 2007 NBA Draft. They took Ohio State center Greg Oden. Durant went second to Seattle. Portland would soon regret the choice. Oden struggled with injuries. The team cut him in 2012. However, he had not played since the 2009–10 season.

Some people disagreed with the NBA's age limit. They believed Durant could have played well in the NBA that year. But Durant was not one of those believers. He said that he was not ready as a person or a player. Durant knew he would soon be rich and famous. But he first wanted to experience college life. Durant learned how to play the national anthem on the piano. He took classes in math, history, and African-American studies. He made new friends. And his confidence grew.

But Durant knew he was ready for the NBA after that one year. And the NBA was ready for him. The Seattle SuperSonics selected him second in the 2007 NBA Draft.

Durant poses with NBA commissioner David Stern after the Seattle SuperSonics selected him in the 2007 NBA Draft.

Kevin Durant

CHAPTER 3

SONIC TO THUNDER

Kevin Durant was excited to finally be in the NBA. But playing in Seattle brought extra pressure. The SuperSonics had struggled in recent years. They also played in an old arena. The team's owner wanted help from the city to build a new arena. He threatened to move the team to Oklahoma City if one was not built. Fans hoped Durant could bring excitement back to Seattle basketball. If so, maybe the city would help build a new arena.

Durant drives to the basket against the Minnesota Timberwolves as a rookie in 2008.

But nobody could save the SuperSonics. They lost 14 of their first 16 games in 2007–08. They lost 14 straight in December and January. Then they lost 15 of 16 in March and April. Even Durant struggled early that year. A nine-game stretch was the low point. Durant had averaged around 11 rebounds per game in college. But he averaged just 3.3 per game during that period. He made just 44 of 137 shots in those games.

It is not uncommon for rookies to struggle like that. NBA players are the biggest, fastest, and most talented in the world. Some players need a few seasons just to adjust. Durant had his ups and downs. But he showed flashes of brilliance as a rookie. And he finished the season on a hot streak. Durant averaged 21.8 points per game in his last 31 games. That helped him earn the Rookie of the Year Award.

Durant helped spark some added interest in the SuperSonics. But it was not enough. The team struggled on and off the court. And the SuperSonics indeed moved to Oklahoma City that summer. The team changed its name to the Oklahoma City Thunder. But the losing continued.

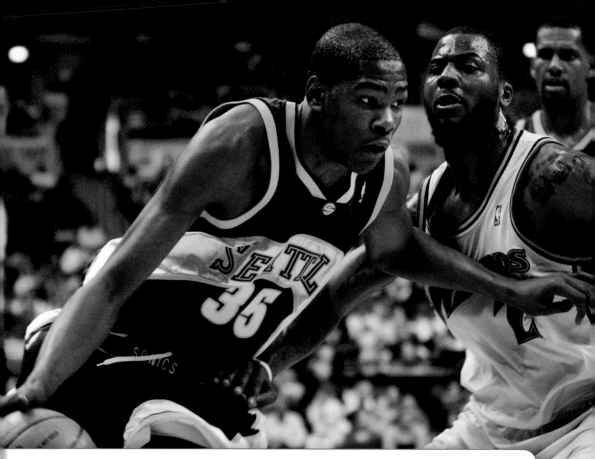

Although he had his ups and downs, Durant played well enough to be named the 2007–08 NBA Rookie of the Year.

The Thunder lost 29 of their first 32 games in 2008–09. There were signs of a bright future, though. The local fans loudly supported the team at home games. And Durant gave them something to cheer about. He had a hot 21-game streak in January and February. He averaged 31 points per game during that time. Durant was quickly proving to be a star player.

Durant and point guard Russell Westbrook, *left*, helped turn the Thunder into winners in Oklahoma City.

Fans had long known of Durant's talent. But Durant knew there was a difference between talent and greatness. The greatest players were not simply the most talented players. Great players helped their teams in many ways—on offense and defense. They also won a lot of games.

But the Thunder finished just 23–59 in Durant's second year. Some thought Durant should have been an All-Star that

Durant has worn No. 35 since his freshman year in college. He chose that number to honor the memory of his first coach, Charles Craig. Craig taught Durant the basics of basketball at the Seat Pleasant Activity Center. Craig was killed in 2005 at the age of 35.

season. But he was not selected. The Thunder's losing record might have hurt his chances. Durant did not complain, though. He said he knew he would need to lead the Thunder to more wins to be an All-Star.

Most believed it would take years to make Oklahoma City a winner. That was not the case, though. Durant and rookie guard Russell Westbrook shined in 2008–09. Rookie guard James Harden then joined the team in 2009–10. They quickly formed a top young trio.

Durant led the way. He attacked the basket with force for points and fouls. He led the NBA with 30.1 points and 10.2 free throw attempts per game. He also made 90 percent of his free throws. The Thunder won 17 of 20 games at one point in early 2010. That helped them finish 50–32. Durant was about to compete in the NBA playoffs for the first time. And he also was about to learn a tough lesson.

Kevin Durant

CHAPTER 4

SOMETHING TO PROVE

The Thunder came into the 2010 NBA playoffs as underdogs. They were the eighth seed. The opposing Los Angeles Lakers were the defending NBA champions. But Durant and his teammates surprised some people.

The Lakers won the first two games of the series. Then the Thunder came back. They won the next two games at home. Fans took notice of the series. The young Thunder were playing the Lakers tough.

Durant flies through the air looking to pass against the Lakers during the 2010 playoffs.

Durant helped Team USA win the 2010 world championship.
It was Team USA's first world title since 1994.

Durant looked like a superstar early on. But he made just 5 of 14 shots in a Game 5 loss. Then he hit only 5 of 23 shots in Game 6. Only two players had shot worse than that in NBA playoffs history. The Thunder were out of the playoffs after that. Durant had made just 43 of 123 shots in the series.

The loss was hard to take for Durant. It was made even harder by his poor performance. But the pain motivated him. Durant was named to the US national team in the off-season. They played in the World Championship. Durant set a tournament record by averaging 22.8 points per game. That helped Team USA win the gold medal. It was Team USA's first world championship since 1994. Durant was named the tournament's Most Valuable Player (MVP).

Team USA played against host Turkey in the championship game. Durant scored 28 points in the 81–64 win. At one point in the game, he hit two straight three-pointers. He pounded his fist to his chest afterward. It was a show of pride. But he refused to toot his own horn after the victory. He instead spoke about the joy he felt about his team winning the gold medal.

Durant only attended the University of Texas for one year. But he had a strong 3.0 grade-point average in college. That is a B average. Durant has since taken summer courses at Texas. He is keeping a promise to his mother that he will earn his college degree.

Durant was ready for the 2010–11 NBA season to start. Fans were eager as well. Many were excited by the young Thunder's play against the Lakers in the previous season's playoffs. Fans wanted to see if the Thunder could take the next step.

Durant improved as a player. He was more consistent. And he led the NBA in scoring for the second straight season. The Thunder finished 55–27 and reached the playoffs. But Durant had learned in 2010 that the playoffs are a different game. The opponents are tougher. The players perform with greater intensity and passion. And they play stronger defense. So it takes more than talent to score—it takes determination.

Durant was ready this time. He averaged 32.4 points per game against the Denver Nuggets in the first round. He twice scored 41 points. The Thunder cruised to a 4–1 series victory.

Durant outplayed the best in the NBA in the 2012 All-Star Game. He scored 36 points. That helped his team to a 152–149 win. Durant was named the All-Star Game MVP for his efforts.

Durant takes a jump shot against the Dallas Mavericks during the 2011 playoffs. The Thunder fell short of the NBA Finals.

Next up were the upstart Memphis Grizzlies. They played the Thunder close. But Durant's big play in Game 7 sent his team to the next round. The Thunder's run finally ended there. The experienced Dallas Mavericks won the series 4–1. Dallas then went on to win the NBA title. But Durant shined in the series. He averaged 28 points and 9.4 rebounds per game.

After leading the Thunder to the 2012 NBA Finals at age 23, the future appears to be bright for Durant.

Durant was well known as an NBA superstar by then. The playoff run confirmed the Thunder were a top team. In fact, many predicted Oklahoma City to win the NBA title in 2011–12. Durant picked up right where he left off. He averaged 28 points per game. That made him the NBA's top scorer for a third straight season. Oklahoma City finished 47–19 and entered the playoffs as the second seed in the Western Conference.

The Thunder then swept past the Mavericks in the first round. Their second round series was against the Lakers. Oklahoma City had a better record that season. But many believed the Lakers had an edge due to their previous playoff success. This series was about the future, though. Durant and the Thunder won in five games. Then they came back to beat the San Antonio Spurs in six games in the conference finals.

The NBA Finals proved to be a tough test. The Miami Heat had three superstars in LeBron James, Dwyane Wade, and Chris Bosh. They had nearly won the title in 2011. Still, the Thunder struck first. Durant tied his 2012 playoff high with 36 points in a Game 1 victory. But Miami turned it up after that. The Heat won the next four games and the title.

Durant was disappointed. But he was also just 23 years old. In just a few short seasons he had blossomed into one of the NBA's best players. He had also surprised many by leading his team to the NBA Finals so quickly. It seemed only a matter of time before Kevin Durant would take the next step.

FUN FACTS AND QUOTES

- Mothers usually say nice things about their sons. But Kevin Durant's mother, Wanda Pratt, really praised her son. "He has the purest heart that I've ever seen in any person," she said in 2010. "He is just a sweet, sweet human being."

- Durant showed his honesty when he turned down an offer to promote the shoe company Adidas. He later signed a contract for less money with Nike. Why did he reject the higher offer from Adidas? Because he had always worn Nike shoes and believed it would be dishonest.

- One of the most fun moments for Durant fans came in the H-O-R-S-E competition during the 2010 NBA All-Star Weekend. The game features players trying to match trick shots. If one player makes a shot, the other has to match it. Durant had already won the event in 2009. He won his battle against Boston Celtics guard Rajon Rondo in 2010 by hitting eight three-pointers in nine attempts.

- Durant's favorite food is crab legs. His favorite ice cream flavor is strawberry. His favorite television show is *Entourage*. His favorite movie is *Twister*. His favorite rap musician is the Notorious B.I.G.

WEB LINKS

To learn more about Kevin Durant, visit ABDO Publishing Company online at **www.abdopublishing.com**. Web sites about Durant are featured on our Book Links page. These links are routinely monitored and updated to provide the most current information available.

GLOSSARY

assist
A pass that directly results in a scored basket.

draft
An annual event in which the top college and international basketball players are selected by NBA teams.

fundamentals
Basic principles.

overtime
An extra period of basketball if the game remains tied after regulation play.

point guard
A position on a basketball team greatly responsible for handling and passing the ball.

rebound
Getting control of the ball after a missed shot.

rookie
A first-year player in the NBA.

scholarship
Financial assistance awarded to students to help them pay for school. Top athletes earn scholarships to represent a college through its sports teams.

varsity
The main team that represents a school.

INDEX

FURTHER RESOURCES

Frager, Ray. *Oklahoma City Thunder*. Edina, MN: ABDO Publishing Co., 2012.

Grange, Michael. *Basketball's Greatest Stars*. Richmond Hill, ON: Firefly Books, 2010.

Silverman, Drew. *Basketball*. Minneapolis, MN: ABDO Publishing Co., 2012.